The #2022 Mediterranean
Diet Cookbook

Tasty and Healthy Dishes incl. Breakfast, Lunch, Dinner, Snacks & More

Morgan Parkins

ISBN - 9798781948581

Table of Contents

EXCLUSIVE BONUS

40 Weight Loss Recipes

&

14 Days Meal Plan

Scan the QR-Code and receive
the FREE download:

What is the Mediterranean Diet?

The Mediterranean diet is centred around the foods that are eaten in Mediterranean countries that border the Mediterranean Sea, such as Spain, France, Greece, and Italy.

The word 'diet' is often associated with an extreme or unenjoyable way of eating. However, although it is called a 'diet', the Mediterranean diet is not a stereotypical diet that you might follow for weight loss. Instead, it is a way of living and forms a key part of the healthy Mediterranean lifestyle.

The Mediterranean diet varies depending on which specific country you're looking at, but each region follows the same basic principles, as detailed below.

What Are the Basics of the Mediterranean Diet?

Often, a diagrammatic triangle or pyramid is used to represent the general 'rules' of the Mediterranean diet.

Foods to Eat

The base of the pyramid indicates the foods that make up a large part of the diet and includes
- Fruits
- Vegetables
- Whole grains
- Nuts
- Beans
- Legumes

The top portion of the pyramid represents the foods and drinks that are consumed in lower amounts, and this includes
- Poultry
- Fish
- Healthy fats, such as those found in olive oil
- Some dairy products, such as eggs, cheese, and yoghurt
- Water
- Wine

The apex of the pyramid shows the foods that are eaten in very small amounts, such as red meats and sweets.

Many diagrams of the Mediterranean diet also include a section for physical activity and social eating at the very base of the triangle.

Foods to Avoid

The things to avoid in the Mediterranean diet include highly processed foods that contain large amounts of saturated fats, sugar, or salt. It's also recommended that you avoid any packaged products with a long list of ingredients that you can't read or have never heard of.

The Basics of Following the Mediterranean Diet

The Mediterranean diet follows several basic principles, including the following.

1. Eat high volumes of fruits, vegetables, beans, legumes, and whole grains. Since the base of the Mediterranean diet pyramid consists of all of these foods, it's important to consume each of them in every meal. Aim to include a range of different types of each category to maximise your nutrient intake and keep your diet fun and varied.
2. Consume lots of healthy fats, including both monounsaturated fatty acids and polyunsaturated fatty acids by replacing butter with olive oil, and eating lots of nuts and seeds.
3. Eat moderate amounts of dairy and eggs, such as eggs, milk, and yoghurt. Dairy is healthy in small doses, as it can help to provide essential nutrients and strengthen bones. It can also lower the risk of cardiovascular disease, metabolic syndrome, obesity, and type 2 diabetes. However, it should not be consumed in

every single meal if you're following the Mediterranean diet. Aim to include dairy products in two of your three daily meals.

4. Limit your intake of red meats and, instead, eat lots of lean meats, such as poultry and fish. Consumption of red meat has been linked to the increased risk of heart disease and poor digestive health. In the Mediterranean diet, red meat should be eaten no more than twice a week.

5. Eliminate highly processed foods. Reduce the amount of fast food and takeaway food you consume. Even better, eliminate them from your diet altogether. Instead, cook your own meals and snacks from scratch using healthy ingredients. It's also important to limit the amount of packaged or pre-made ready meals that you eat.

6. Drink lots of water and occasionally drink red wine. Water keeps you hydrated and aids digestion. Red wine contains resveratrol that reduces oxidative damage and inflammation in the body. You should also keep your consumption of high-calorie or high-sugar drinks to a minimum.

7. Share your food with others. In Mediterranean countries, mealtimes are seen as a sociable event and sharing food with your loved ones is thought to contribute to the many incredible health benefits of the diet. Be deliberate and mindful when you eat, and share your portions amongst those around you.

Top Tips to Following the Mediterranean Diet

Here are some quick tips to make the Mediterranean diet much easier for you to stick to.

- Build your meals around plant-based foods, particularly vegetables, beans or legumes, and whole grains
- Eat fish at least twice a week

- When frying or cooking your food, use olive oil instead of butter
- Avoid highly processed foods
- Consume red meat no more than once a week
- Stay physically active and practice regular movement
- Enjoy socialising with your friends and family during mealtimes and enjoy yourself!

Why Did the Mediterranean Diet Gain Popularity?

The Mediterranean diet initially gained popularity back in the 1950s because researchers noticed that those who lived in Mediterranean countries, and, therefore, followed a Mediterranean diet seemed to have a lower incidence of heart disease.

Since then, further research has confirmed that the Mediterranean diet can promote good health, extend lifespan, and reduce the risk of heart attacks, strokes, type 2 diabetes, and premature death.

Benefits of the Mediterranean Diet

There are several amazing benefits to following the Mediterranean diet.

Reduced Risk of Disease

There's a reason that the Mediterranean diet is known for being extremely healthy. The combination of amazing compounds in the various foods that Mediterranean countries eat can lower your risk of getting multiple diseases. In particular, the Mediterranean diet is known to decrease the chances of heart disease, stroke, and type 2 diabetes.

Improved Physical and Mental Health

Since this Mediterranean diet focuses largely on fruits and vegetables, it provides all the essential micronutrients (vitamins and minerals), as well as lots of fibre, all of which contribute to your overall health and well-being. Vitamins and minerals are required by the body for optimal growth, development, and metabolism. The healthy fibre boosts your digestion and feeds the good bacteria in your gut.

It's not just your physical health that benefits from the Mediterranean diet. Your mental health can get a huge boost as well!

The positive effects that this diet has on your gut health can lead to increased serotonin within the body, which can leave you feeling happier and more motivated. The healthy fats in the diet can enhance brain health and cognitive function, which can further boost your mental health.

Improved Heart Health

High levels of triglycerides in the blood can lead to inflammation, hardening of the arteries, and thickening of the artery walls, a condition known as atherosclerosis. Alongside triglycerides, low-density lipoproteins ('bad' cholesterol) cause the artery walls to become sticky, meaning cholesterol deposits more easily along the insides of the arteries.

However, the healthy fats (omega-3 and omega-6 fatty acids) that are provided with the Mediterranean diet have cardioprotective effects. They help to reduce the levels of triglycerides and low-density lipoproteins in the blood. In turn, this lowers the chances of atherosclerosis, blood clots, stroke, and heart attacks.

Lower Risk of Stroke or Thrombosis

Stroke and thrombosis occur when the blood sticks together and forms a clot that gets stuck in one of your arteries or veins. This can be extremely dangerous as it blocks the flow of blood through the vessels.

The fatty fish and olive oil in the Mediterranean diet contains omega-3 and omega-6 fatty acids. These polyunsaturated fats can help to reduce the stickiness of the blood, which reduces blood clotting.

Nuts and seeds also contain monounsaturated and polyunsaturated fatty acids that can enhance these health benefits.

Reduced Inflammation

Inflammation is known to contribute to several different diseases in the body, such as heart disease, cancer, digestive disorders, arthritis, and autoimmune conditions.

The high levels of polyunsaturated fats in the Mediterranean diet can help to reduce this inflammation and reduce your risk of developing these conditions.

Extended Lifespan

The Mediterranean diet advocates drinking small amounts of red wine.

The grapes used to make red wine contain a compound called resveratrol. This is a polyphenol obtained from plants that have been shown to extend lifespan in animal models. It acts as an antioxidant in the body and helps to reduce oxidative damage to cells.

It may also lower the risk of cancer development due to its antitumour activity. Research shows that it can prevent cancer growth at various stages of carcinogenesis.

Why You Should Love the Mediterranean Diet

Aside from the amazing health benefits that the Mediterranean diet provides, there are lots of other reasons to love it!

Firstly, there's no calorie counting involved. The Mediterranean diet focuses on consuming lots of healthy foods as opposed to focusing on the numbers. Because the diet is centred around vegetables, fruits, legumes, and whole grain carbohydrates, you are able to eat a high volume of food whilst also maintaining your weight.

The Mediterranean diet is full of fresh and delicious foods. Each meal you cook will be full of colour and flavour, whether it's a salad, a soup, or a pasta dish.

Unlike many other diets, the Mediterranean diet doesn't limit or completely remove certain food groups. Many diets will emphasise the need to eat low amounts of carbohydrates or fats, which can restrict the meals and snacks that you're able to eat. However, the Mediterranean diet consists of all food groups and does not demonise carbs or fats!

It also includes an array of tasty herbs and spices that will keep your meals interesting and varied.

Because of the wide array of different ingredients that you can use in your recipes, you will never get bored of the Mediterranean diet. It's much more than a Greek salad or an Italian pizza! The possibilities are endless...

There's no doubt that you're going to feel satisfied and satiated when you start following the Mediterranean diet. With the rich-tasting foods, flavoursome seasoning, and moderate amounts of wine, you won't feel restricted at all. It won't feel like you're on a diet, but you will still gain all of the incredible benefits of living a healthy lifestyle.

Who Can Follow the Mediterranean Diet?

Just because you don't live in a Mediterranean country, it doesn't mean you can't follow the Mediterranean diet! Everybody can experience the physical and mental health benefits of following this diet. If you're unsure whether it's going to work for you, try it out for yourself and see how you feel after a few months.

To help you get started with trying out the Mediterranean diet, The #2022 Mediterranean Diet Cookbook is packed full of delicious and healthy recipes that will provide you with great meals and snacks for weeks to come.

This book contains tasty recipes for breakfast, lunch, dinner, sides, snacks, and desserts using ingredients in accordance with the Mediterranean diet. Every recipe is easy to follow and contains lots of fresh ingredients. Serving sizes and nutritional information is included with every recipe so you can track your food intake quickly and easily.

EXCLUSIVE BONUS

40 Weight Loss Recipes

&

14 Days Meal Plan

Scan the QR-Code and receive
the FREE download:

Recipes

Breakfast

Mediterranean Breakfast Bowls

Makes 4 servings
Preparation time – 10 minutes
Cooking time – 15 minutes
Nutritional value per serving – 267 kcals, 9 g carbs, 16 g protein, 9 g fat

Ingredients

♦ 4 eggs
♦ 1 tbsp olive oil
♦ 200 g / 7 oz button mushrooms, halved
♦ 200 g / 7 oz cherry tomatoes
♦ 200 g / 7 oz fresh spinach
♦ 2 garlic cloves, peeled and minced
♦ ¼ tsp salt
♦ ¼ tsp black pepper
♦ 8 tbsp hummus
♦ 4 tbsp olives

Method

1. Place the eggs in a pan of cold water so that each egg is covered by an inch or two of water.
2. Bring the water to boil before turning it down to a simmer. Cook the eggs on a low heat for 8-12 minutes.
3. Strain the water from the pan and pour cold water over the eggs to cool them down quickly. Place one egg in each bowl.
4. Heat the olive oil in a frying pan and add the mushrooms. Cook until browned (around 10 minutes)
5. Add the cherry tomatoes, spinach, garlic cloves, salt, and black pepper to the pan and cook for a further 2-3 minutes until the spinach begins to wilt.
6. Divide the mixture evenly into each bowl.
7. Spoon 2 tbsp of hummus into each bowl, followed by 1 tbsp olives.
8. Enjoy your Mediterranean bowls for breakfast!

Greek Granola Yoghurt Pots

Makes 4 servings
Preparation time – 5 minutes
Cooking time - none
Nutritional value per serving – 199 kcals, 10 g carbs, 15 g protein, 12 g fat

Ingredients

- ♦ 400 g / 14 oz rolled oats
- ♦ 100g raw mixed nuts, chopped
- ♦ 1 tsp ground cinnamon
- ♦ 4 tbsp honey
- ♦ 4 tbsp coconut oil
- ♦ 800 g / 28 oz full-fat Greek yoghurt
- ♦ 400 g / 14 oz frozen berries (strawberries, raspberries, and blueberries)

Method

1. Preheat the oven to 170 degrees Celsius / 350 degrees Fahrenheit.
2. To make the granola, place the oats, nuts, and cinnamon in a bowl.
3. Pour in the honey and coconut oil.
4. Mix until fully combined, making sure all of the oats are fully covered by the honey and oil.
5. Place some greaseproof paper on an oven tray and spread the granola mixture evenly across the tray.
6. Bake for 22 minutes, stirring halfway through.
7. While the granola is cooking, prepare the yoghurt pots by placing 200g of Greek yoghurt into each bowl.
8. Top each bowl with 100g berries.
9. When the granola has browned and the oats are crispy, remove them from the oven and allow to cool for a few minutes before sprinkling evenly into each bowl.
10. Store any extra granola in an airtight container at room temperature.

Greek Pumpkin Parfait

Makes 4 servings
Preparation time – 5 minutes
Cooking time - none
Nutritional value per serving – 143 kcals, 18 g carbs, 6 g protein, 4 g fat

Ingredients

- 200 g / 7 oz pumpkin puree
- 400 g / 14 oz full-fat Greek yoghurt
- 3 tbsp mascarpone cheese
- 1 tbsp vanilla extract
- 2 tbsp brown sugar
- 2 tsp ground cinnamon
- 1 tsp ground nutmeg
- 2 tbsp mixed nuts, chopped

Method

1. Place all of the ingredients in a bowl, except the mixed nuts.
2. Mix the ingredients together using a spoon or a hand blender until it forms a smooth, consistent mixture.
3. Serve the parfait mixture evenly into four bowls, cover, and fridge for 30-60 minutes.
4. Remove from the fridge and top with the mixed nuts when you're ready to eat.

Mediterranean Vegetable Frittata

Makes 8 servings
Preparation time – 15 minutes
Cooking time – 30 minutes
Nutritional value per serving – 172 kcals, 6 g carbs, 12 g protein, 10 g fat

Ingredients

- 1 red bell pepper, sliced
- 1 zucchini, diced
- 1 onion, sliced
- 200 g / 7 oz broccoli
- 1 tbsp olive oil
- ½ tsp salt
- 8 eggs, beaten
- ½ tsp baking powder
- 200 ml cow's milk
- 80 g / 3 oz feta cheese
- 1 tsp fresh herbs (any kind)

Method

1. Preheat the oven to 220 degrees Celsius / 450 degrees Fahrenheit.
2. Place the pepper, zucchini, onion, broccoli, and salt in a large bowl.
3. Pour in the olive oil and mix until most of the vegetables are covered.
4. Bake the vegetables on a lined baking tray for 15 minutes until they have turned crispy and slightly brown.
5. Turn the oven down to 180 degrees Celsius / 400 degrees Fahrenheit.
6. In a bowl, mix the eggs, baking powder, milk, cheese, and herbs until fully combined.
7. Transfer the mixture into a small casserole dish or quiche dish.
8. Cook in the oven for 10 minutes until the frittata is firm and crispy on top.
9. Serve up with a fresh side salad and an extra drizzle of olive oil.

Greek Bougatsa with Homemade Custard Filling

Makes 8 servings
Preparation time – 15 minutes
Cooking time – 1 hour
Nutritional value per serving – 250 kcals, 15 g carbs, 9 g protein, 13 g fat

Ingredients

For the custard

- 100 g / 3.5 oz wholemeal flour
- 4 eggs, beaten
- 200 g / 7 oz sugar
- 500 ml milk
- 1 tsp vanilla extract
- 1 tsp ground cinnamon
- 2 tbsp pistachios

For the bougatsa

- 10 sheets filo pastry
- 200 g / 7 oz unsalted butter, melted

Method

1. Start by making the custard filling by combining the flour, sugar, and eggs in a heatproof bowl. Whisk until fully combined.

2. Pour the milk, vanilla extract, and cinnamon into a saucepan and bring to a near boil. Just before the milk boils, pour one-third of it into the flour mixture. Stir to combine.

3. Turn the heat down before adding the flour and milk mixture to the remaining two-thirds of milk in the saucepan.

4. Whisk immediately to combine the ingredients for 2-3 minutes until the mixture thickens and becomes smooth and creamy. Keep the saucepan on the stove while doing this. Set aside to cool.

5. For the bougatsa, preheat the oven to 170 degrees Celsius / 350 degrees Fahrenheit and line a baking tin with greaseproof paper.

6. Place 6 sheets of filo pastry in the baking tin to cover the bottom in an even layer. Baste each one with melted butter.

7. Pour the custard mixture over the top of the filo pastry sheets until they are covered, but not soaked.

8. Fold the sides of the filo pastry layer over the custard mixture to ensure it doesn't leak out.

9. Top with the remaining 4 sheets of filo pastry and, again, top each one with melted butter.

10. Score each sheet of filo pastry with a knife and bake in the oven for 45 minutes until the pastry is golden and crispy.

11. Serve warm with an extra sprinkle of cinnamon or icing sugar.

The 'Eggs, Onion, and Tomato' Bake

Makes 4 servings
Preparation time – 10 minutes
Cooking time – 20 minutes
Nutritional value per serving – 234 kcals, 19 g carbs, 14 g protein, 11 g fat

Ingredients

- 200 g / 7 oz cherry tomatoes, halved
- 2 tbsp red wine vinegar
- 2 onions, sliced
- 4 tbsp olive oil
- 4 cloves garlic, peeled and minced
- ½ tsp salt
- ½ tsp black pepper
- 4 eggs

Method

1. Toss together the tomatoes with the red wine vinegar in a bowl.
2. Heat 1 tbsp olive oil in a large, flat frying pan and cook the onion and garlic for 10 minutes until softened and fragrant.
3. Add the tomatoes, salt, and black pepper to the pan and cook for a further 2-3 minutes.
4. Using a spoon, press down in four areas of the pan to create small coves.
5. Crack the eggs into each cove and continue cooking until each egg is cooked to your liking.
6. Serve up for a delicious breakfast!

Honey and Fig Overnight Oats

Makes 4 servings
Preparation time – 10 minutes
Refrigeration time – 8 hours
Nutritional value per serving – 212 kcals, 24 g carbs, 8 g protein, 13 g fat

Ingredients

♦ 280 g / 10 oz rolled oats
♦ 200 ml water
♦ 100 ml milk (any type)

♦ 2 tbsp dried figs, chopped
♦ 2 tbsp mixed nuts, chopped
♦ 2 tbsp honey

Method

1. Combine all of the ingredients in a bowl. If you need to add more water, do so now.
2. Cover the bow and fridge overnight for 8 hours.
3. The next morning when you're ready to eat, remove the oats from the fridge and serve up with your favourite toppings.

Fig and Ricotta Toast

Makes 2 servings
Preparation time – 20 minutes
Cooking time – 3 minutes
Nutritional value per serving – 267 kcals, 13 g carbs, 7 g protein, 8 g fat

Ingredients

- 2 slices crust wholegrain bread
- 60 g / 2 oz ricotta cheese
- 1 fresh fig or 2 dried figs, sliced
- 1 tbsp sliced almonds
- 1 tsp honey

Method

1. Toast the wholegrain bread to your liking.
2. Spread the ricotta cheese evenly across the toast and top with the figs, almonds, and a drizzle of honey.
3. Eat immediately while the toast is still warm.

Mixed Berry Chia Seed Pudding

Makes 2 servings
Preparation time – 5 minutes
Refrigeration time – 8 hours
Nutritional value per serving – 313 kcals, 13 g carbs, 7 g protein, 16 g fat

Ingredients

- 100 g / 3.5 oz blackberries
- 100 g / 3.5 oz raspberries
- 200 ml milk (any type)
- 8 tbsp chia seeds
- 2 tbsp maple syrup
- 1 tsp vanilla extract
- 100 ml Greek yoghurt
- 50 g / 1.7 oz granola

Method

1. Place the blackberries, raspberries, and milk in a blender until they form a smooth, consistent mixture.
2. Transfer the mixture into a bowl and stir in the chia seeds, syrup, and vanilla extract until combined.
3. Cover and refrigerate overnight for 8 hours.
4. Serve up the next morning into 2 bowls and top with half of the granola each.
5. Store any leftovers in the fridge for up to 3 days.

Baked Banana and Walnut Oatmeal Muffins

Makes 8 servings
Preparation time – 15 minutes
Cooking time – 25-30 minutes
Nutritional value per serving – 203 kcals, 26 g carbs, 9 g protein, 6 g fat

Ingredients

♦ 400 g / 14 oz rolled oats
♦ 200 ml cow's milk
♦ 2 ripe bananas, mashed
♦ 2 eggs, beaten
♦ 4 tbsp walnuts, chopped
♦ 1 tsp baking powder
♦ 1 tsp nutmeg
♦ 1 tsp cinnamon
♦ 1 tsp vanilla extract

Method

1. Preheat the oven to 170 degrees Celsius / 350 degrees Fahrenheit.
2. Place muffin cases into a 12-cup muffin tray.
3. Combine all of the ingredients in a bowl and stir until it forms a consistent mixture.
4. Divide the mixture evenly into the 12 muffin cases.
5. Bake in the oven for 25-30 minutes until the muffins are cooked all the way through. This can be tested by inserting a knife into the centre. If cooked, it will come out dry.
6. Once cooked, remove from the oven and serve warm.

Baked Omelette Muffins

Makes 4 servings
Preparation time – 20 minutes
Refrigeration time – 6 hours
Nutritional value per serving – 209 kcals, 16 g carbs, 5 g protein, 14 g fat

Ingredients

- 1 tbsp olive oil
- 4 bacon, chopped
- 100 g / 3.5 oz broccoli, chopped
- 2 sticks celery, finely sliced
- 2 onions, finely sliced
- 50 g / 1.7 oz cherry tomatoes
- 8 eggs
- 100 g / 3.5 oz cheddar cheese, grated
- 100 ml cow's milk
- ½ tsp salt
- ½ tsp black pepper

Method

1. Preheat the oven to 170 degrees Celsius / 350 degrees Fahrenheit.
2. Grease a 12-cup muffin tray with a small bit of the olive oil.
3. Heat the rest of the olive oil in a large skillet on a medium heat. Add the bacon and cook for 5 minutes until it is cooked and slightly browned.
4. Remove from the pan and place on some paper towels.
5. Add the chopped broccoli, celery, onions, and tomatoes to the pan and cook for 5-6 minutes until the vegetables have slightly softened.
6. Whisk the eggs, cheese, milk, salt, and black pepper in a bowl until fully combined. Mix in the bacon and vegetables.
7. Divide the mixture evenly into the 12 muffin cups.
8. Bake for 20-30 minutes until the eggs are firm and fully cooked.

Mediterranean Breakfast Fruit Smoothie

Makes 1 serving
Preparation time – 5 minutes
Cooking time – none
Nutritional value per serving – 265 kcals, 30 g carbs, 12 g protein, 9 g fat

Ingredients

♦ 100 g / 3.5 oz frozen strawberries

♦ 100 g / 3.5 oz frozen raspberries

♦ 1 ripe banana, chopped

♦ 200 ml milk (any type)

♦ 1 tbsp peanut butter

♦ 1 tbsp chia seeds

Method

1. Combine all of the ingredients in a blender.
2. Pulse until a smooth and consistent mixture forms.
3. Serve up in a glass and enjoy!

Lunch

Mediterranean Style Fruit Salad

Makes 4 servings
Preparation time – 10 minutes
Cooking time – 10 minutes
Nutritional value per serving – 149 kcals, 12 g carbs, 9 g protein, 5 g fat

Ingredients

- 100 g / 3.5 oz dry whole wheat couscous
- ½ pineapple, dice
- 4 tangerines, segmented
- 2 tbsp honey
- 1 tbsp olive oil
- 2 tbsp flaked almonds

Method

1. Place the couscous in a pan and add enough water to cover the couscous by around 1-1.5 inches. Add the lid to the pan.
2. Bring the water to a boil before turning down to a simmer and cooking the couscous for 5-10 minutes until most of the water has been absorbed.
3. Set the couscous aside to cool for a few minutes before spooning the couscous across the bottom of four bowls.
4. Place the pineapple chunks and tangerine segments on top of the couscous.
5. Drizzle the honey and olive oil over the fruit, followed by the flaked almonds.
6. Enjoy your Mediterranean style fruit salad for lunch!

Mediterranean Chicken Quinoa Bowl

Makes 4 servings
Preparation time – 20 minutes
Cooking time – 10 minutes
Nutritional value per serving – 149 kcals, 12 g carbs, 9 g protein, 5 g fat

Ingredients

- 400 g / 14 oz boneless, skinless chicken breast, sliced
- 2 red bell peppers, sliced
- 1 clove garlic, peeled and crushed
- ½ white onion, sliced
- 4 tbsp flaked almonds
- 3 tbsp olive oil
- 1 tsp paprika
- ½ tsp ground cumin
- 2 tbsp olives
- 200 g / 7 oz dry quinoa
- 50 g / 1.7 oz feta cheese, grated
- 2 tbsp fresh parsley, finely chopped

Method

1. Cook the quinoa according to packet instructions.
2. Preheat the oven to 170 degrees Celsius / 350 degrees Fahrenheit.
3. Line a baking tray with some greaseproof paper.
4. Place the sliced chicken evenly on the baking tray and cook in the oven for 15 minutes.
5. Add the peppers, garlic, onion, almonds, 2 tbsp olive oil, paprika, cumin in a blender and pulse until it forms a smooth puree.
6. Combine the quinoa, olives, 1 tbsp olive oil in a bowl and stir to combine. Divide evenly into four bowls.
7. Split the pepper puree over the quinoa in each bowl.
8. Top with the cooked chicken, feta cheese, and parsley.

Tabouli Salad

Makes 4 servings
Preparation time – 10 minutes
Cooking time – none
Nutritional value per serving – 65 kcals, 5 g carbs, 2 g protein, 5 g fat

Ingredients

♦ 100 g / 3.5 oz uncooked extra fine bulgur wheat
♦ 4 cherry tomatoes, finely chopped
♦ 1 cucumber, sliced
♦ 4 spring onions, finely chopped
♦ ½ tsp salt
♦ ½ tsp black pepper
♦ 2 tbsp fresh parsley, chopped
♦ 12 mint leaves, stems removed, washed, and finely chopped
♦ 3 tbsp olive oil
♦ 2 tbsp lemon juice or lime juice

Method

1. Wash the bulgur wheat and place in a bowl. Cover with cold water and allow to soak for 5-7 minutes. Drain well.

2. Place the cherry tomatoes, cucumber, and spring onions in a bowl. Add the soaked bulgur wheat and season with ½ tsp salt and ½ tsp black pepper.

3. Stir in the fresh parsley and mint leaves, followed by the olive oil and lemon or lime juice.

4. Serve up in a bowl for lunch or as a side to your main dish.

Greek Mezze Bowl

Makes 4 servings
Preparation time – 30 minutes
Cooking time – 10 minutes
Nutritional value per serving – 378 kcals, 29 g carbs, 27 g protein, 16 g fat

Ingredients

- 200 g / 7 oz quinoa, dry
- 400 g / 14 oz ground turkey
- 200 g / 7 oz frozen spinach
- 80 g / 3 oz feta cheese
- ½ tsp garlic powder
- ½ tsp dried oregano
- ½ tsp salt
- ½ tsp black pepper
- 2 tbsp olive oil
- 2 tbsp lemon juice
- 2 tbsp fresh parsley, chopped
- 12 cherry tomatoes
- 1 cucumber, sliced
- 1 red bell pepper, sliced
- 4 tbsp tzatziki

Method

1. Cook the quinoa according to the packet instructions. Once cooked, leave to cool in a bowl.
2. Combine the ground turkey, spinach, feta, garlic powder, oregano, salt, and black pepper in a bowl until it forms one homogenous mixture.
3. Spoon out small pieces of the mixture and roll into around 12 balls.
4. Heat 1 tbsp olive oil in a frying pan and cook the meatballs for 10-12 minutes until they are cooked all the way through, and the outside is crispy and brown.
5. Set the meatballs aside to drain on some paper towels.
6. Stir the 1 tbsp olive oil, lemon juice, and fresh parsley into the quinoa.
7. Divide the quinoa into 4 bowls and top each serving with 3 meatballs.
8. Add 3 cherry tomatoes, and some cucumber and red pepper slices to the bowls, followed by a dollop of tzatziki.
9. Enjoy with some pitta bread!

Avgolemono Soup

Makes 4 servings
Preparation time – 10 minutes
Cooking time – 50 minutes
Nutritional value per serving – 287 kcals, 30 g carbs, 18 g protein, 6 g fat

Ingredients

- 2 boneless, skinless chicken breast
- 1 tbsp olive oil
- 100 g / 3.5 oz carrots, finely sliced
- 100 g / 3.5 oz celery, finely chopped
- 100 g / 3.5 oz spring onion, finely chopped
- 2 garlic cloves, peeled and minced
- 4 chicken stock cubes
- 2 bay leaves
- 200 g / 7 oz uncooked wholegrain rice
- ½ tsp salt
- ½ tsp black pepper
- 1 lemon
- 2 eggs, beaten
- 1 tbsp fresh parsley, chopped

Method

1. Preheat the oven to 200 degrees Celsius / 400 degrees Fahrenheit and line a baking tray with a sheet of greaseproof paper.
2. Place the chicken breast on the tray and bake in the oven for 20 minutes until cooked and golden.
3. Shred the chicken into a bowl and set aside.
4. Heat 1 tbsp olive oil in a large saucepan over a low to medium setting, and add the carrots, celery, spring onion, and garlic. Saute for 3-5 minutes until the vegetables begin to soften.
5. Dissolve the chicken stock cubes according to the packet instructions and pour into the saucepan. Add the bay leaves to the pan and increase the heat to a high setting.
6. Once the liquid comes to a boil, add the rice, salt, and pepper, and cover the pan with the lid.
7. Meanwhile, prepare the sauce by whisking together the juice 1 lemon and eggs in a bowl. Add two tbsp of hot broth to the egg mixture and stir to combine.
8. Pour the hot egg mixture into the saucepan and stir to combine. Remove from the heat almost immediately.
9. Serve the soup while still hot with a sprinkle of fresh parsley alongside a crusty bread roll.

Roasted Red Pepper Soup

Makes 4 servings
Preparation time – 10 minutes
Cooking time – 50 minutes
Nutritional value per serving – 187 kcals, 14 g carbs, 3 g protein, 4 g fat

Ingredients

♦ 6 red bell peppers, sliced
♦ 4 cloves garlic, peeled
♦ 1 1/2 tbsp olive oil
♦ 1 onion, sliced
♦ 6 sundried tomatoes
♦ 2 vegetable stock cubes
♦ 1/2 tsp salt
♦ 1/2 tsp black pepper
♦ 1 tbsp crème fraiche

Method

1. Preheat the oven to 200 degrees Celsius / 400 degrees Fahrenheit.
2. Line a baking tray with greaseproof paper and place the red bell peppers and garlic cloves evenly across the tray.
3. Drizzle a small amount of olive oil (around 1 tsp) over the top of the peppers and garlic, and roast in the oven for 40 minutes.
4. Heat the remaining olive oil in a pan and sauté the onion until soft and translucent (around 8-10 minutes).
5. Add the roasted peppers and garlic, as well as the sun-dried tomatoes to the pan and cook for a further 2 minutes.
6. Transfer the mixture to a large saucepan and add the salt and pepper.
7. Dissolve the vegetable stock cubes according to the packet instructions and pour into the saucepan.
8. Bring the mixture to a boil and simmer for 10 minutes until heated through.
9. Serve up with some crème fraiche on top.

Spanakopita (Spinach Pies)

Makes 4 servings
Preparation time – 10 minutes
Cooking time – 10 minutes
Nutritional value per serving – 476 kcals, 65 g carbs, 29 g protein, 3 g fat

Ingredients

- 450 g / 16 oz chopped spinach, thawed
- 2 handfuls fresh parsley, finely chopped
- 1 onion, finely chopped
- 2 garlic cloves, peeled and minced
- 3 tbsp olive oil
- 4 eggs, beaten
- 250 g / 8 oz feta cheese, crumbled
- 1/2 tsp black pepper
- 450 g / 16 oz filo pastry sheets

Method

1. Preheat the oven to 150 degrees Celsius / 300 degrees Fahrenheit.
2. Drain the spinach and squeeze out any excess liquid.
3. In a bowl, mix the spinach, parsley, onion, garlic cloves, 2 tbsp olive oil, beaten eggs, and crumbled feta until fully combined.

4. Line a baking tray with a small amount of olive oil or some greaseproof paper.
5. Roll out 2 of the filo pastry sheets and use a spoon or brush to cover them lightly in some of the remaining 1 tbsp of olive oil. Place another 2 sheets of filo pastry over the top and, again, brush the top of them with olive oil. Repeat this until around two-thirds of the pastry is used up.
6. Evenly spread the spinach mixture across the top of the filo pastry and top with the final third of the filo pastry sheets and brush with a little oil.
7. Fold the sides of the pastry down so that there are no holes along the sides of the spinach pies.
8. Cut part way through the pies to allow some of the heat to escape during the cooking process.
9. Bake in the oven for 45-60 minutes until the filo pastry is golden and crispy.
10. Remove from the oven and finish cutting the pie into even squares.
11. Serve up with a side salad and some tzatziki.

Greek Chicken and Yoghurt Sauce Pitta

Makes 4 servings
Preparation time – 70 minutes
Cooking time – none
Nutritional value per serving – 100 kcals, 7 g carbs, 5 g protein, 7 g fat

Ingredients

♦ 1 tbsp lemon juice

♦ 3 tsp olive oil

♦ 1 tsp dried oregano

♦ 2 tbsp garlic, minced

♦ 400 g / 14 oz boneless, skinless chicken breast

♦ 100 ml Greek yoghurt

♦ 2 tsp fresh mint, chopped

♦ 1 tsp black pepper

♦ 4 whole wheat pitta breads

♦ 1 cucumber, sliced

♦ 100 g / 7 oz fresh lettuce, chopped

♦ 100 g / 7 oz plum tomatoes, halved

Method

1. Combine the lemon juice, 2 tsp olive oil, dried oregano, and minced garlic in a bowl and whisk together.
2. Chop the chicken into small pieces and add to the bowl. Toss to coat with the lemon and oil mixture.
3. Marinate in the fridge for 1 hour.
4. Preheat the oven to 200 degrees Celsius / 400 degrees Fahrenheit and place greaseproof paper on a baking tray.
5. Remove the chicken from the fridge and place evenly on the baking tray. Bake in the oven for 12-15 minutes until fully cooked.
6. In the meantime, mix the Greek yoghurt, mint, and black pepper in a bowl.
7. Halve the pitta breads and spread the yoghurt mixture evenly across one half of each pitta bread.
8. Place the chicken in the pitta alongside some cucumber, lettuce, and plum tomatoes.
9. Serve warm or cold.

Slow Cooker Mediterranean Soup

Makes 4 servings
Preparation time – 20 minutes
Cooking time – 4 hours
Nutritional value per serving – 450 kcals, 31 g carbs, 29 g protein, 13 g fat

Ingredients

- 200 g / 7 oz dried chickpeas, soaked overnight
- 600 ml water
- 1 onion, finely chopped
- 4 garlic cloves, finely chopped
- 100 g / 3.5 oz cherry tomatoes, chopped
- 2 tbsp tomato paste
- 4 tsp cayenne pepper
- 4 tbsp paprika
- ½ tsp black pepper
- 400 g / 14 oz boneless, skinless chicken
- 2 sticks celery, chopped
- 2 tbsp fresh parsley, chopped

Method

1. Drain the chickpeas and add them to the slow cooker alongside 600 ml water.
2. Add all of the other ingredients to the slow cooker, except the fresh parsley.
3. Place the lid on the slow cooker and turn it onto a high heat for 4 hours or a low heat for 8 hours.
4. Once cooked, turn the slow cooker off and serve up the soup with a sprinkle of fresh parsley on top.

Chicken and Edamame Greek Salad

Makes 4 servings
Preparation time – 30 minutes
Cooking time – none
Nutritional value per serving – 450 kcals, 31 g carbs, 29 g protein, 13 g fat

Ingredients

- 400 g / 14 oz boneless, skinless chicken breast
- 2 tbsp vinaigrette
- 2 tbsp olive oil
- ½ tsp salt
- ½ tsp black pepper
- 200 g / 7 oz edamame beans
- 100 g / 3.5 oz feta cheese
- ½ onion, sliced
- 100 g / 3.5 oz cherry tomatoes, halved
- ½ cucumber, sliced
- 1 tbsp dried chives

Method

1. Place the chicken in a saucepan and add enough water to cover it by 1-2 inches.

2. Bring the water to a boil before turning the heat down to a simmer and cook for 12-15 minutes.

3. Transfer the chicken to a chopping board and shred into small pieces.

4. In a bowl, mix the vinaigrette, olive oil, salt, and black pepper together.

5. Add the chicken, edamame, feta, onion, tomatoes, cucumber, dried chives to the bowl and mix until all of the ingredients are coated in the sauce.

6. Serve up the salad on its own or as a side dish.

Dinner

Chicken Shawarma

Makes 8 servings
Preparation time – 3 hours 10 minutes
Cooking time – 30 minutes
Nutritional value per serving – 412 kcals, 30 g carbs, 16 g protein, 6 g fat

Ingredients

- ½ tbsp ground cumin
- ½ tbsp turmeric powder
- ½ tbsp garlic powder
- ½ tbsp paprika
- ½ tsp cayenne pepper
- 8 boneless, skinless chicken breast fillets
- 1 onion, sliced
- 8 cherry tomatoes, whole
- Juice 1 lemon
- 150 g / 5 oz wholegrain rice, uncooked
- 2 tbsp tzatziki

Method

1. In a bowl, mix the cumin, turmeric, garlic, paprika, and cayenne pepper until combined.
2. Add the chicken breasts to the bowl and toss to coat. Refrigerate for 3 hours.
3. Preheat the oven to 200 degrees Celsius / 400 degrees Fahrenheit.
4. Remove the chicken from the fridge and place on a lined baking tray alongside the onion.
5. Drizzle the juice of 1 lemon over the top of the chicken, onions, and whole cherry tomatoes.
6. Roast for 30 minutes until the chicken is slightly brown and crispy on top.
7. Meanwhile, bring a saucepan of water (around 175-200 ml) to boil and cook the rice for 18-20 until has absorbed most of the water and is soft to touch.
8. Serve the chicken alongside the rice and tzatziki for dinner.

Baked Fish with Lemon Garlic Sauce

Makes 2 servings
Preparation time – 10 minutes
Cooking time – 10 minutes
Nutritional value per serving – 230 kcals, 2 g carbs, 21 g protein, 7 g fat

Ingredients

- 2 tbsp butter
- 2 tbsp olive oil
- 3 garlic cloves, peeled and chopped
- 1 lemon
- 400 g / 14 oz white fish fillets
- ½ tsp salt
- ½ tsp black pepper
- 1 tsp fresh parsley, chopped

Method

1. Preheat the oven to 200 degrees Celsius / 400 degrees Fahrenheit.
2. In a frying pan, heat the butter and oil. Add the garlic and cook for 1-2 minutes.
3. Add the zest of the lemon to the pan and stir.
4. Thinly slice the lemon and place them at the bottom of a baking tray that is lined with oil or greaseproof paper.
5. Place the fish on top of the lemons and add the salt and pepper.
6. Use a spoon or brush to baste the fish on both sides with the garlic butter.
7. Bake the fish for 10-12 minutes in the oven until it is cooked through. It should easily fall apart with a fork.
8. To serve, sprinkle the fresh parsley on top.

Falafel

Makes 6 servings
Preparation time – 18 hours 15 minutes
Cooking time – none
Nutritional value per serving – 100 kcals, 7 g carbs, 5 g protein, 7 g fat

Ingredients

- 400 g / 14 oz dried chickpeas
- ½ tsp baking powder
- 1 onion, chopped
- 4 garlic cloves, peeled and chopped
- 2 tbsp fresh parsley, chopped
- 2 tbsp fresh coriander, chopped
- 1 tbsp ground black pepper
- 1 tbsp ground cumin
- 1 tsp cayenne pepper
- 1 tsp baking powder
- 2 tbsp toasted sesame seeds
- 1 tbsp olive oil
- 6 whole wheat pitta breads
- 2 tbsp hummus
- 1 cucumber, sliced
- 6 cherry tomatoes, halved
- Handful lettuce, rinsed

Method

1. Place the chickpeas in a bowl and fill with cold water until the chickpeas are covered by around 2 inches. Leave them to soak overnight for at least 18 hours. If the chickpeas are still hard after this time, continue to soak for a few more hours. The chickpeas should be soft to touch.

2. Add the chickpeas, onion, garlic, parsley coriander, black pepper, cumin, and cayenne pepper to a food processor and pulse until combined. It should form a smooth, consistent mixture that is free of large lumps.

3. Spoon out small parts of the falafel mixture and roll into 12 small balls.

4. Place the sesame seeds in a bowl and roll each falafel ball into the seeds to coat.

5. Heat the oil in a large frying pan and cook 6 balls at a time for 3-5 minutes until the outer coating is brown and crispy.

6. Once cooked, set aside to cool.

7. Cut the whole wheat pitta breads in half and spread the hummus across one half of each. Place the cucumber, tomatoes, and lettuce in the wrap.

8. Chop the falafel balls in half and place four halves in each wrap to serve.

Shakshuka

Makes 4 servings
Preparation time – 10 minutes
Cooking time – 30 minutes
Nutritional value per serving – 194 kcals, 12 g carbs, 9 g protein, 8 g fat

Ingredients

- 1 tbsp olive oil
- 1 onion, sliced
- 2 green bell peppers, sliced
- 2 cloves garlic, peeled and sliced
- 1 tsp ground coriander
- 1 tsp ground cumin
- 1/2 tsp salt
- 1/2 tsp black pepper
- 6 beef tomatoes, sliced
- 4 tbsp tomato paste
- 4 eggs, whole
- 2 tbsp fresh parsley, chopped

Method

1. Heat the oil in a large skillet. Add the onion, peppers, garlic, ground coriander, ground cumin, salt, and pepper, and cook for 5-6 minutes until the vegetables begin to soften.

2. Add the tomatoes and tomato pasta, cover with the lid, and allow to simmer for 15 minutes. Add a little more salt and pepper if necessary.

3. Using a spoon, make 4 indentations in the tomato mixture and crack an egg into each one.

4. Reduce the heat to a gentle simmer and cook for a further 8-10 minutes until the egg whites are fully cooked and set.

5. Serve up with some fresh parsley sprinkled on top.

Baked Halibut

Makes 4 servings
Preparation time –15 minutes
Cooking time – 30 minutes
Nutritional value per serving – 387 kcals, 9 g carbs, 18 g protein, 27 g fat

Ingredients

For the sauce

- 2 lemons
- 2 tbsp olive oil
- 2 garlic cloves, peeled and chopped
- 2 tsp dried oregano
- 1 tsp salt
- ½ tsp black pepper
- 1 tsp ground coriander

For the fish

- 300 g / 10 oz green beans, chopped
- 300 g / 10 oz cherry tomatoes
- 1 onion, sliced
- 400 g / 14 oz halibut fish, diced

Method

1. Preheat the oven to 230 degrees Celsius / 450 degrees Fahrenheit.

2. In a bowl, whisk together the sauce ingredients until combined.

3. Toss the green beans, tomatoes, and onion and tomatoes in the sauce before using a spoon or spatula to remove them.

4. Line a baking tray with greaseproof paper and spread the coated vegetables across half of the tray.

5. Add the fillets to the sauce and toss to coat. Place the halibut next to the vegetables on the baking tray.

6. Pour the remaining sauce over the top of the fish and vegetables.

7. Bake in the oven for 25-30 minutes until the fish is cooked. It should fall apart when you lift it.

8. Serve warm alongside some wholegrain rice or pasta.

Shrimp and Garlic Pasta

Makes 4 servings
Preparation time – 10 minutes
Cooking time – 10 minutes
Nutritional value per serving – 476 kcals, 65 g carbs, 29 g protein, 3 g fat

Ingredients

◆ 200 g / 7 oz spaghetti,
uncooked
◆ ½ tsp salt
◆ 2 tbsp olive oil
◆ 400 g / 14 oz shrimp, peeled
and deveined
◆ 4 garlic cloves, peeled and
minced
◆ 1 tsp dry oregano
◆ 1 tsp red pepper flakes
◆ 200 ml white wine
◆ 1 lemon
◆ 4 vine tomatoes, chopped
◆ 30 g / 1 oz Parmesan cheese,
grated

Method

1. Boil a saucepan of water and add the pasta along with a touch of salt. Cook the pasta for 10-12 minutes or according to the packet instructions.

2. Meanwhile, heat 1 tbsp olive oil in a large wok or frying pan and cook the shrimp for 2-3 minutes until it turns pink. Once cooked, set aside.

3. Heat the other 1 tbsp olive oil in the same pan and add the onion, garlic, oregano, and red pepper flakes. Cook for 2 minutes before adding the white wine to the pan and cooking for a further 1-2 minutes.

4. Add the juice and zest of the lemon into the pan, followed by the chopped vine tomatoes.

5. Stir the pasta and shrimps into the pan and allow to heat for a couple of minutes.

6. To serve, sprinkle some grated cheese on top of the shrimp pasta and serve immediately while the food is still warm.

Italian Baked Chicken

Makes 4 servings
Preparation time – 15 minutes
Refrigeration time – 30 minutes
Nutritional value per serving – 199 kcals, 10 g carbs, 14 g protein, 5 g fat

Ingredients

♦ 400 g / 14 oz boneless,
skinless chicken breast

♦ 1 tsp salt

♦ 1 tsp black pepper

♦ 2 tsp dried oregano

♦ 2 tsp fresh thyme

♦ 1 tsp smoked paprika

♦ 4 cloves garlic, peeled and
minced

♦ 1 red onion, sliced

♦ 6 vine tomatoes, halved

♦ 2 tbsp olive oil

♦ 2 tbsp feta cheese, crumbled

♦ 1 tbsp fresh parsley,
chopped

Method

1. Preheat the oven to 230 degrees Celsius / 450 degrees Fahrenheit.
2. Place the chicken in a sandwich bag and place on the kitchen worktop. Use a mallet to flatten the chicken breast.
3. Remove the chicken from the sandwich bag and place in a bowl. Sprinkle a little salt and black pepper on both sides of each breast.
4. Add the oregano, thyme, smoked paprika, and minced garlic to the bowl and toss to coat the chicken.
5. Line a baking tray with greaseproof paper and scatter the onion evenly across the tray. Place the chicken breasts on top along with the tomatoes.
6. Drizzle 2 tbsp olive oil over the top of the ingredients and bake in the oven for 20 minutes.
7. After 20 minutes, remove the chicken from the oven and sprinkle the crumbled feta on top of both breasts. Return to the oven for a further 10 minutes until the chicken is fully cooked and golden on top.
8. Serve the chicken immediately with some fresh parsley on top. Enjoy with some wholegrain rice or freshly made tomato sauce on top.

Moroccan Vegetable Tagine

Makes 4 servings
Preparation time – 18 hours 15 minutes
Cooking time – 1 hour
Nutritional value per serving – 475 kcals, 55 g carbs, 21 g protein, 17 g fat

Ingredients

- 200 g / 7 oz chickpeas, dried and uncooked
- 2 tbsp olive oil
- 2 onions, sliced
- 8 cloves garlic, peeled and chopped
- 2 medium sweet potatoes, peeled and diced
- 2 carrots, peeled and sliced
- 1 tbsp harissa spice blend
- 1 tsp ground turmeric
- 1 tsp ground cinnamon
- 1 tsp dried parsley
- 60 g / 2 oz dried apricots
- 1 x 400 g / 14 oz can chopped plum tomatoes
- 1 vegetable stock cube, dissolved
- 1 lemon

Method

1. Place the chickpeas in a large bowl and add enough cold water to cover them by 1-2 inches. Cover with a dry towel and leave to soak overnight for at least 18 hours or until the chickpeas are soft to touch.
2. In a large wok or frying pan, heat the olive oil and sauté the onions for 5-6 minutes until they begin to soften.
3. Add the garlic, sweet potato, and carrots to the pan, and sprinkle the harissa spice blend, ground turmeric, ground cinnamon, and dried parsley over the top.
4. Cook on a medium to high heat for 7-8 minutes, stirring regularly.
5. Add the dried apricots, plum tomatoes, and dissolved vegetable stock cube into the pan,
6. Continue cooking for a further 10 minutes on a medium to high heat before turning it down to a low heat and simmering for 20-25 minutes.
7. Stir in the chickpeas and add the juice of 1 lemon. Allow to heat through for 5 minutes and add extra spices if desired.
8. Serve immediately with some Moroccan style couscous and enjoy (see below for the Moroccan couscous recipe).

Sides and Snacks

Greek Side Salad

Makes 1 serving
Preparation time – 10 minutes
Cooking time – none
Nutritional value per serving – 100 kcals, 7 g carbs, 5 g protein, 7 g fat

Ingredients

♦ 100 g / 3.5 oz fresh lettuce
♦ 1 cucumber, sliced
♦ 4 cherry tomatoes, halved
♦ ½ red onion, sliced
♦ 1 tbsp feta cheese, crumbled
♦ 1 tbsp olive oil
♦ 2 tsp vinaigrette

Method

1. Place the lettuce, cucumber, tomatoes, onion, and feta cheese in a bowl.
2. Drizzle the olive oil and vinaigrette over the top.
3. Enjoy as a side to your main meal or eat alongside some pitta bread and hummus to enjoy for lunch.

Moroccan Style Couscous

Makes 4 servings
Preparation time – 10 minutes
Cooking time – 20 minutes
Nutritional value per serving – 219 kcals, 19 g carbs, 4 g protein, 7 g fat

Ingredients

♦ 2 tbsp olive oil

♦ ½ onion, sliced

♦ 2 garlic cloves, peeled and minced

♦ ½ tsp ground cumin

♦ ½ tsp ground cinnamon

♦ 2 vegetable stock cubes

♦ 350 g / 12 oz couscous, uncooked

♦ 50 g / 2 oz raisins

♦ 50 g / 2 oz sliced almonds, toasted

♦ 1 tbsp fresh parsley, chopped

Method

1. Heat the olive oil in a large saucepan on a medium to high heat and add the onion, garlic, cumin, and cinnamon. Cook for 5 minutes until the onion becomes translucent and soft.
2. Dissolve the vegetable stock cubes according to the packet instructions and add to the pan. Cover the pot with the lid and bring to a boil.
3. Allow the mixture to boil for 1-2 minutes before removing from the heat and stirring in the couscous.
4. Set aside for 10-15 minutes to allow the couscous to absorb the stock.
5. Stir in the raisins, almonds, and fresh parsley.
6. Serve alongside some Moroccan tagine or a Greek salad.

Italian Roasted Vegetables

Makes 4 servings
Preparation time – 10 minutes
Cooking time – 30 minutes
Nutritional value per serving – 78 kcals, 13 g carbs, 4 g protein, 3 g fat

Ingredients

- 8 button mushrooms, rinsed and halved
- 400 g / 14 oz new potatoes, rinsed and halved
- 400 g / 14 oz cherry tomatoes
- 2 zucchini, diced
- 10 cloves garlic, peeled and sliced
- 1 tbsp olive oil
- ½ tsp dried oregano
- ½ tsp dried thyme
- ½ tsp salt
- ½ tsp black pepper
- 50 g / 2 oz parmesan cheese, grated

Method

1. Preheat the oven to 230 degrees Celsius / 450 degrees Fahrenheit and line a baking tray with a sheet of tinfoil.
2. Place the mushrooms, new potatoes, cherry tomatoes, zucchini, and garlic in a large mixing bowl. Add the oil and toss to coat all of the vegetables.
3. Transfer the vegetables onto the baking tray and spread so they form an even layer. Sprinkle the dried oregano, dried thyme, salt, and pepper over the top.
4. Bake for 20 minutes until the vegetables are cooked and crispy on top.
5. Serve immediately with the parmesan cheese sprinkled on top.

Greek Chicken Souvlaki with Homemade Tzatziki

Makes 4 servings
Preparation time – 2 hours 30 minutes
Cooking time – 15 minutes
Nutritional value per serving – 280 kcals, 13 g carbs, 17 g protein, 7 g fat

Ingredients

For the souvlaki

- 10 garlic cloves, peeled
- 2 tbsp dried oregano
- 1 tsp dried rosemary
- 1 tsp paprika
- ½ tsp salt
- ½ tsp black pepper
- 2 tbsp olive oil
- 100 ml dry white wine
- 1 lemon
- 1 bay leaf
- 400 g / 14 oz boneless, skinless chicken breast, sliced

For the tzatziki

- ½ cucumber, peeled and sliced
- 4 garlic cloves, peeled and minced
- 1 tsp white vinegar
- 1 tbsp olive oil
- 400 g / 14 oz Greek yoghurt

Method

1. Place the garlic, oregano, rosemary, paprika, salt, pepper, olive oil, white wine, and juice 1 lemon, in a food processor.
2. Pulse until fully combined.
3. Place the chicken in a bowl along with the bay leaf. Pour the marinade over the top and toss until all of the chicken is covered.
4. Place in the fridge for 2 hours.
5. Meanwhile, make the tzatziki by adding the cucumber to a food processor and blending until shredded.
6. Remove the cucumber and place on a dry tea towel.
7. In a bowl, mix the garlic, white vinegar, and olive together. Add the cucumber and stir in the yoghurt. Store in the fridge until ready to serve.
8. Preheat the oven to 200 degrees Celsius / 400 degrees Fahrenheit and line a baking tray with greaseproof paper.
9. Place the chicken pieces evenly along 8 wooden skewers and place the skewers on the baking tray.
10. Cook in the oven for 15 minutes, turning halfway through, until the chicken is fully cooked and golden.
11. Serve the chicken with a side of wholewheat pitta bread, homemade tzatziki, and Greek salad.

Greek Lemon Rice

Makes 4 servings
Preparation time – 20 minutes
Cooking time – 20 minutes
Nutritional value per serving – 145 kcals, 16 g carbs, 4 g protein, 8 g fat

Ingredients

♦ 200 g / 7 oz uncooked long
  grain rice
♦ 1 tbsp olive oil
♦ 1 onion, chopped
♦ 1 garlic clove, peeled and
  minced
♦ 2 lemons
♦ 2 chicken or vegetable stock
  cubes
♦ ½ tsp salt
♦ 1 tbsp fresh parsley,
  chopped

Method

1. Rinse the rice and place in a bowl. Cover with cold water and leave to soak for 15 minutes until it turns soft.
2. Heat 1 tbsp olive oil in a saucepan and add the onions and garlic. Sauté for 3-4 minutes until the onions turn slightly translucent and begin to soften.
3. Dissolve the stock cubes according to the packet instructions and pour into the pan alongside the juice of 2 lemons.
4. Add the rice to the pan and stir to combine.
5. Bring to a boil and then turn the heat to a low setting. Cover with the lid and leave to cook for 20 minutes until the rice has absorbed most of the stock.
6. Remove from the heat and set aside to cool for 10 minutes.
7. Add the fresh parsley and serve as a side dish for dinner.

Greek Yoghurt and Honey Pot

Makes 1 serving
Preparation time – 5 minutes
Cooking time – none
Nutritional value per serving – 179 kcals, 10 g carbs, 15 g protein, 6 g fat

Ingredients

♦ 100 g / 7 oz Greek yoghurt

♦ 1 tsp chia seeds

♦ 1 tsp pumpkin seeds

♦ 1 tbsp honey

Method

1. Place the Greek yoghurt in a bowl and top with the chia seeds and pumpkin seeds.

2. Drizzle the honey over the top and enjoy!

Yoghurt Ice Cream

Makes 4 servings
Preparation time – 4 hours 15 minutes
Cooking time – 20 minutes
Nutritional value per serving – 234 kcals, 19 g carbs, 14 g protein, 11 g fat

Ingredients

♦ 300 ml milk

♦ 100 ml single cream

♦ 1 tbsp honey

♦ 100 g / 3.5 oz brown sugar

♦ 1 tsp vanilla extract

♦ 300 g / 10 oz Greek yoghurt

Method

1. Mix the milk, single cream, honey, sugar, and vanilla extract in a saucepan and place on a low to medium heat.

2. Remove from the heat and set aside to cool for a few minutes. When the mixture reaches room temperature, stir in the yoghurt.

3. Allow the mixture to set for at least 4 hours.

4. Pour the mixture into an ice cream maker and set on a low speed for 20 minutes.

5. Once complete, place in the freezer.

6. Serve with some fruit or cake for dessert.

Honey, Almond, and Ricotta Spread

Makes 4 servings
Preparation time – 10 minutes
Cooking time – 45 minutes
Nutritional value per serving – 74 kcals, 9 g carbs, 5 g protein, 8 g fat

Ingredients

♦ 100 ml ricotta cheese spread
♦ 100 g / 3.5 oz sliced almonds, toasted
♦ ½ tsp almond extract
♦ 1 tsp honey

Method

1. Place all of the ingredients in a bowl and mix to combine.
2. Serve as a side dip to your favourite dish or spread on a piece of wholemeal toast for lunch.

Garlic Hummus

Makes 8 servings
Preparation time – 10 hours 15 minutes
Cooking time – none
Nutritional value per serving – 101 kcals, 9 g carbs, 6 g protein, 3 g fat

Ingredients

- 200 g / 7 oz uncooked chickpeas
- 2 garlic cloves, peeled
- 1 tbsp olive oil
- 2 tbsp tahini
- 2 tbsp lemon juice
- ½ tsp cayenne pepper
- 1 tbsp fresh parsley, chopped

Method

1. Place the dry chickpeas in a bowl and pour in enough water to cover the chickpeas by 1-2 inches. Cover with a dry towel and leave to soak overnight until the chickpeas are soft to touch.

2. Place the chickpeas and the rest of the ingredients into a food processor and pulse until a smooth mixture forms. If the mixture looks a little dry, add some cold water.

3. Serve the hummus as a side dish or on top of some hot pitta bread.

Tahini Sauce

Makes 4 servings
Preparation time – 10 minutes
Cooking time – none
Nutritional value per serving – 65 kcals, 5 g carbs, 2 g protein, 5 g fat

Ingredients

- 1 garlic clove, peeled and minced
- 1/2 tsp salt
- 150 ml tahini paste
- 1/2 tbsp lime juice
- 2 tbsp fresh parsley, chopped

Method

1. Place all of the ingredients into a food processor and pulse until blended.
2. Add enough water to turn the mixture into a smooth paste and continue to pulse until combined.
3. Transfer the tahini into a bowl and serve as a side dish alongside your main meal.

Desserts

Granola Bars

Makes 8 servings
Preparation time – 15 minutes
Cooking time – 20 minutes
Nutritional value per serving – 289 kcals, 34 g carbs, 12 g protein, 8 g fat

Ingredients

- 400 g / 14 oz rolled oats
- 100 g / 3.5 oz mixed nuts, chopped
- 4 tbsp sunflower seeds
- 4 tbsp chia seeds
- 2 tbsp honey
- 100 g / 3.5 oz sultanas
- 2 tbsp cashew butter
- 1 tsp vanilla extract

Method

1. Preheat the oven to 170 degrees Celsius / 350 degrees Fahrenheit.
2. Place all of the ingredients in a bowl and stir to combine.
3. Grease a baking tin with a small amount of olive oil or line with some greaseproof paper.
4. Pour the mixture into the baking tin and spread evenly so that the top layer is smooth.
5. Bake in the oven for 20 minutes until the top has turned golden.
6. Remove from the oven and set aside on a cooling rack for at least 10 minutes.
7. Cut into squares and serve up warm or cold. Store any leftovers in the fridge for up to 5 days.

Crunchy Quinoa Bars

Makes 20 servings
Preparation time – 5 minutes
Cooking time – 10 minutes
Nutritional value per serving – 156 kcals, 20 g carbs, 7 g protein, 16 g fat

Ingredients

♦ 200 g / 7 oz quinoa,
   uncooked
♦ 200 g / 7 oz dark chocolate
♦ 200 g / 7 oz milk chocolate
♦ 1 tsp vanilla extract
♦ 2 tbsp crunchy peanut
   butter

Method

1. Cook the quinoa according to the packet instructions. Once cooked, set aside.
2. Place the chocolate in a small heatproof bowl.
3. Heat a small saucepan of water on the hob and place the bowl containing the chocolate on top so that the bowl is sitting just above the water.
4. Heat, constantly stirring, until the chocolate has fully melted.
5. Pour the melted chocolate into the quinoa and add the vanilla extract and peanut butter. Stir until fully combined.
6. Line a baking tin with greaseproof paper and pour the mixture into the tin. Spread the top so that it forms an even layer.
7. Place the quinoa bars in the fridge to set for 1-2 hours.
8. Serve warm or cold with an extra drizzle of peanut butter on top.

Baklava

Makes 8 servings
Preparation time – 45 minutes
Cooking time – 40 minutes
Nutritional value per serving – 179 kcals, 23 g carbs, 10 g protein, 14 g fat

Ingredients

For the syrup

- 400 g / 14 oz sugar
- 2 cardamom pods
- 2 tbsp ground cinnamon
- 2 tbsp honey
- 2 tbsp lemon juice

For the baklava

- 300 g / 10 oz pistachios, walnuts, almonds, or a mixture of all three
- 100 g / 3.5 oz sugar
- 30 sheets filo pastry
- 100 g / 3.5 oz salted butter, melted
- ½ tsp ground cinnamon

Method

1. To make the syrup, fill a small saucepan with water and bring to a boil. Stir in the sugar, cardamom pods, and cinnamon, and stir to combine.

2. Simmer for 15 minutes until the mixture thickens slightly. Remove from the heat and stir in the honey and lemon juice. Place in the fridge until ready to serve.

3. For the baklava, add the nuts to a food processor and pulse until they form a coarse mixture of small pieces.

4. Pour the nuts into a bowl and stir in the sugar until combined.

5. Preheat the oven to 180 degrees Celsius / 350 degrees Fahrenheit and line a baking tray with some olive oil or greaseproof paper.

6. Place down 10 of the filo pastry sheets along the bottom of the tray, one at a time. Brush each one with some melted butter.

7. Evenly spread one half of the nut mixture across the filo pastry and cover with 10 more sheets, buttering each one as above.

8. Top with the other half of the nut mixture and finish with the final 10 sheets of filo pastry, again, buttering each one as you go along.

9. Cut off the edges of the pastry along the sides of the dish.

10. Using a sharp knife, cut the baklava into triangles or squares.

11. Bake the baklava in the oven for 30-40 minutes until each one is golden and crispy.

12. Remove from the oven and serve with a drizzle of syrup on top. Store any leftovers in the fridge.

Lemon Cake

Makes 8 servings
Preparation time – 10 minutes
Cooking time – 45 minutes
Nutritional value per serving – 223 kcals, 28 g carbs, 6 g protein, 12 g fat

Ingredients

For the cake

- 400 ml sweetened almond or soya milk
- 1 lemon
- 100 g / 3.5 oz sugar
- 2 tbsp olive oil
- 400 g / 14 oz wholewheat flour
- 1 tsp baking powder
- ½ tsp salt

For the glaze

- 200 g / 7 oz powdered sugar
- 2 tbsp lemon juice
- 1 tsp vanilla extract

Method

1. Preheat the oven to 180 degrees Celsius / 350 degrees Fahrenheit and line a loaf tin with greaseproof paper.
2. Whisk the milk in a bowl along with the zest and juice of 1 lemon. Set aside.
3. In a bowl, mix the sugar and olive oil until combined. Stir in the milk and lemon mixture.
4. Place the flour, baking soda, and salt in a bowl before folding in the wet ingredients.
5. Pour the batter into the lined loaf tin and smooth out the top so it forms an even layer.
6. Bake in the oven for 45 minutes until fully cooked through. Test this by inserting a dry knife into the centre of the cake. It should come out clean.
7. Set the cake aside on a cooling rack whilst you make the glaze.
8. In a bowl, whisk together the powdered sugar, lemon juice, and vanilla extract until combined.
9. Pour the glaze over the cool cake and serve warm or cold with a sprinkle of sugar and lemon juice on top.

Kataifi

Makes 20 servings
Preparation time – 30 minutes
Cooking time – 1 hour
Nutritional value per serving – 299 kcals, 22 g carbs, 4 g protein, 17 g fat

Ingredients

For the syrup

- 450 g / 16 oz sugar
- 300 ml water
- 1 lemon
- 2 tbsp ground cinnamon

For the kataifi

- 250 g / 9 oz walnuts, chopped (almonds or pistachios can be used instead)
- 1 tsp ground cinnamon
- 450 g / 16 oz kataifi dough
- 200 g / 7 oz butter, melted

Method

1. To make the syrup, place all of the ingredients into a saucepan and bring to a boil. As soon as the sugar starts to dissolve, the syrup is ready. Set aside to cool.

2. Meanwhile, prepare the kataifi filling by placing the walnuts and cinnamon in a blender. Pulse until it forms a coarse mixture.

3. Preheat the oven to 180 degrees Celsius / 350 degrees Fahrenheit and line a square or rectangular baking tin with greaseproof paper.
4. Roll out the kataifı dough and tear into shreds to create a fluffy dough.
5. Take one piece of kataifı dough and spread it on the work surface. Drizzle 1 tbsp melted butter on one end of the dough followed by 1 tbsp of the nut filling.
6. Roll the dough up tightly to form a small cylinder.
7. Place the kataifı roll in the lined baking tin and brush with some more of the melted butter.
8. Repeat this process until all of the kataifı rolls have been placed in the pan and all of the nut mixture has been used. Make sure there are no gaps between the rolls in the baking tin.
9. Bake the kataifı rolls in the oven for 1 hour until golden and crispy.
10. Remove from the oven and drizzle the homemade syrup on top. Set aside to allow the kataifı dough to absorb the syrup.
11. Serve with a little more syrup and a side of ice cream or custard.

Fig and Almond Cake

Makes 8 servings
Preparation time – 45 minutes
Cooking time – 40 minutes
Nutritional value per serving – 283 kcals, 33 g carbs, 8 g protein, 17 g fat

Ingredients

♦ 2 tbsp lemon juice

♦ 3 tbsp honey

♦ 2 tbsp olive oil

♦ 2 eggs, beaten

♦ 1 tsp salt

♦ 300 g / 10 oz almond flour

♦ 1 tsp baking powder

♦ 10 fresh figs, sliced

Method

1. Preheat the oven to 180 degrees Celsius / 350 degrees Fahrenheit and line a cake tin with greaseproof paper.
2. In a bowl, whisk together the lemon juice, honey, olive oil, eggs, and salt.
3. Fold in the almond flour and baking powder and stir until combined.
4. Pour the batter into the lined cake tin and top with the fig slices.
5. Bake for 30-40 minutes until the cake is cooked through and the top is golden. Test whether the cake is cooked by inserting a clean knife into the centre. It will come out dry when the cake is ready.
6. Set aside to cool before cutting into slices.
7. Serve hot or cold for dessert.

Chocolate Ganache with Raspberry Shortbread

Makes 8 servings
Preparation time – 4 hours 30 minutes
Cooking time – 40 minutes
Nutritional value per serving – 441 kcals, 30 g carbs, 7 g protein, 20 g fat

Ingredients

For the shortbread

- 100 g / 3.5 oz sugar
- 150 g / 5 oz butter, melted
- 1 egg plus 1 egg yolk
- 1 tsp almond extract
- 200 g / 7 oz wholewheat flour

For the raspberry caramel

- 150 g / 5 oz raspberries
- 100 ml single cream
- 200 g / 7 oz sugar
- 2 tbsp honey
- 1 tbsp salted butter

For the ganache

- 200 g / 7 oz double cream
- 200 g / 7 oz milk or dark chocolate
- 50 g / 2 oz salted butter, melted

Method

1. To make the shortbread, mix the sugar and melted butter until it forms a light fluffy mixture.
2. Whisk in the egg and egg yolk, followed by the almond extract.
3. Fold in the flour and mix to form a dough.
4. Place the dough in the fridge for 4 hours to set.
5. Preheat the oven to 180 degrees Celsius / 300 degrees Fahrenheit and line a cake tin with greaseproof paper.
6. Transfer the dough into the lined cake tin and bake for 30 minutes.
7. Meanwhile, make the raspberry caramel by placing the raspberries in a food processor and pulsing until soft and mushy.
8. Remove the raspberries from the blender and place them into a bowl. Stir in the cream and set the mixture aside.
9. In a saucepan, heat the sugar and honey until it starts to caramelize.
10. Pour the raspberries into the saucepan in two halves to ensure it doesn't overspill. Turn onto a low heat and heat for 2-3 minutes before setting aside to cool to room temperature.
11. Remove the dough from the oven and carefully pour the raspberry mixture over the top.

12. To make the ganache, break apart the chocolate into a heat proof bowl.

13. Heat the cream in a saucepan over a low heat until it comes to a boil.

14. Pour the hot cream into the bowl of chocolate. Allow the cream to melt the chocolate pieces for a few minutes as you whisk the ingredients together.

15. Once the chocolate pieces have fully melted, add the butter, and stir until fully combined.

16. Pour the chocolate ganache over the raspberry tart and store in the fridge until ready to serve.

17. Serve cold with a side of ice cream or a drizzle of single cream.

EXCLUSIVE BONUS

40 Weight Loss Recipes

&

14 Days Meal Plan

Scan the QR-Code and receive
the FREE download:

Disclaimer

This book contains opinions and ideas of the author and is meant to teach the reader informative and helpful knowledge while due care should be taken by the user in the application of the information provided. The instructions and strategies are possibly not right for every reader and there is no guarantee that they work for everyone. Using this book and implementing the information/recipes therein contained is explicitly your own responsibility and risk. This work with all its contents, does not guarantee correctness, completion, quality or correctness of the provided information. Misinformation or misprints cannot be completely eliminated.

Printed in Great Britain
by Amazon

78181528R00064